LOST LINES OF ENGLAND
THE CHEDDAR VALLEY LINE

PAUL LAWTON

GRAFFEG

CONTENTS

Foreword	3
Introduction	5
Yatton	12
Congresbury	17
Wrington	22
Sandford & Banwell	24
Axbridge	34
Cheddar	39
Draycott	42
Lodge Hill	44
Wookey	45
Wells	46
Wells Priory Road	50
Shepton Mallet	52
Cranmore	56
Wanstrow	58
Witham	61

2 Lost Lines of England

FOREWORD

The 1960s were a sad time for those who loved the old branch lines and it was even more poignant for those who had spent their lives working on them. It was clear that something we had known for so long was soon to be destroyed without a great deal of thought about what might be needed in the future. Fortunately, there was a rush to capture the scenes on film and in that way preserve a flavour of them for future generations; such pictures have formed the basis for a successful series of books on the lost lines of Wales. The series has now moved into England and it is something of a privilege to write about the line from Yatton to Witham. The information and pictures may add to the enjoyment of those who walk and cycle along the Cheddar Valley trail. It is also hoped that the book will bring back memories for those who knew the line all those years ago and especially for the people who, like the author, grew up with it.

Country branch lines, especially Great Western ones, had a character and charm that was all their own. This was perhaps because they often ran through beautiful countryside that in the 1950s and 60s seemed typical of the West Country as it was at that time. The journey from Yatton began by passing through pastoral levels before hitting the southern edge of the Mendips at Sandford & Banwell. It then skirted the prime strawberry land below the hills of Cheddar, Draycott and Wookey before reaching Wells, England's smallest and most charming city. From there it was a challenging slog of some three miles of 1 in 46 to Shepton Mallet, before another climb to near Cranmore, then finally dropping down through Wanstrow to Witham. The last passenger services ran on 7th September 1963. The Yatton–Cheddar section closed to goods on 1st October 1964 leaving Cheddar–Witham served by a daily diesel-hauled pick-up goods. The section west of Dulcote Quarry (just east of Wells) closed on 26th April 1969 and the bitumen traffic, which had kept the section to Cranmore open, ceased in September 1985. It was left to the East

Somerset Railway's preservation efforts at Cranmore and the massive exports of limestone from Merehead Quarry to keep two sections of the line in use.

Most of the photographs that accompany the text were taken by the author as a young teenager. They were taken on a Voigtlander Vito B 35mm camera lent to him by his grandfather. It had an excellent lens but lacked a light meter, so exposure times depended on guesswork and careful perusal of the little guide that came packed with the film. Film stock in those days could be quite grainy, especially when developed at home. Enlargements were then made in a darkroom set up in a spare bedroom. One mentions these facts to excuse any shortcomings in the images. The other problem with young photographers is that they are not always as careful at keeping records as they might be, not just of exposure times but even of train times. Likewise, dates and even locations were consigned to oblivion. After the passage of so many years the latter was a particular challenge when selecting the images for inclusion in the book. The advantage the pictures have is that those taken by the author have never before been published.

INTRODUCTION

Like many railways, especially those in rural areas that were constructed in the second great wave of railway building in the 1860s, the Yatton to Witham route was a line made up of two halves, produced by two different companies. They were constructed at different times and from different ends. They met in Wells and helped give that small cathedral city one of the most convoluted railway histories that any community of that size could be expected to achieve, or indeed tolerate. No fewer than three stations were built in Wells. The first was opened by the Somerset Central Railway in Priory Road on 3rd March 1859 as the terminus of its branch from Glastonbury. By then the idea of connecting the prosperous and productive area of central Somerset with the outside world had begun to attract other railway companies and the usual machinations began. While the Bristol & Exeter Railway and the Somerset & Dorset (successor of the SCR) tried to outmanoeuvre one another, the East Somerset Railway stole a march by beginning the construction of the eastern section of our route. The ESR built a broad-gauge single line from Witham Friary to Shepton Mallet (opened in 1858) and Wells (opened in 1862). Witham station was on the Wiltshire, Somerset and Weymouth line from Frome to Yeovil that opened in 1856. The line from Witham terminated at a station just east of Priory Road and was planned by no less a luminary than I.K. Brunel. The engineer was Mr Ward and the contractor Rowland Brotherhood of Chippenham. Both the B&E and the S&D had nurtured plans to approach Wells from the west, thus completing the Yatton–Witham line. In the end it made financial sense to reach an agreement and it was left to the B&E to make the final connection into Wells. Construction of the Cheddar Valley line from Yatton began in March 1867.

The B&E section to Wells was planned by Francis Fox, the railway's Chief Engineer and his brother John, both of whom had been educated at Sidcot School, the Quaker foundation near Winscombe. Perhaps they already had some doubts about the long-term viability of the broad gauge. They laid the line with cross sleepers instead of placing them longitudinally, as was commonly used on the broad gauge. This meant that when the conversion to standard gauge took place, the changeover was completed in just four days. The brothers decided to begin the engineering work by dealing first with the most formidable obstacle, the tunnel under Winscombe hill. This was the spot chosen for the cutting of the ceremonial 'first sod' by Mrs Anna Yatman of Winscombe Hall on 26th February 1867. For her trouble she was presented with an engraved silver spade and decorated wheelbarrow, which she said would become heirlooms for her children. Ironically, the Yatmans had fled other parts of the country to avoid railway building and then found that a line was to go beneath the new hall they had constructed. It is said that the exuberance of the celebrations rather surprised the two abstemious Quaker brothers. The B&E took the step of appointing a chaplain to cater for the social and moral well-being of the navvies. As usual, the workmen completed their task without causing any serious trouble, thus confounding the fears of many locals. The line was officially opened on 30th August 1869. At 11.00am, a train left Bristol with the directors of the railway and other luminaries conveyed in a special saloon. These included the chairman of the company, the Earl of Devon. Other guests shared a coach with the Brislington band, who played throughout the journey. The train went first to Cheddar, and then returned to Axbridge, where the Brislington band was joined in a parade by the Axbridge workhouse fife and drum band. Two hundred of the poor of the parish were then given 'a substantial dinner of Old English Fare, with a sufficiency of beer'.

The new line prompted varying opinions. The inhabitants of the villages and towns were generally pleased that they were no longer reliant on the speed of a horse for a connection with the outside world. The vicar of Cheddar welcomed it: 'I have been labouring for 33 years against four great enemies – pride, ignorance, bigotry and prejudice. Now the Directors of the railway are coming among the people with their noble line to civilise the whole neighbourhood'. He also congratulated the railway company for not running trains on Sundays, 'by which the Sabbath has been desecrated and the people demoralised'.

Others took a more cautious view. At the half-yearly meeting of the B&E in September 1869, Mr Dallaway of Bath, presumably a shareholder, complained that they 'had opened a line to Cheddar that would never pay, for it was one of the worst lines in England'. Interestingly, there were no Sunday services when closure was proposed in 1963, nor at that point did the line pay. Those who had opposed the line in 1869 on the grounds that it was a desecration of the countryside were soon mollified as nature healed the scars and the line became a very pretty one on which to travel. While the line did not pay once road transport developed, it began well enough. As was often the case, the first station buildings tended to be temporary. Commercially the line showed such early promise that more permanent structures were required and in this area the B&E excelled. The wooden structures were replaced by ones in Mendip stone with superb and very distinctive decorative bargeboards and roofs. In November 1875, the track was converted from broad to standard gauge and the line became part of the Great Western Railway the following year.

At this point Wells had three stations within half a mile of one another with no rails connecting them. The Board of Trade would not accept the laying of mixed-gauge track to complete the connection and the impecunious ESR was not able to countenance paying for the conversion to standard gauge. The ESR was not a flourishing concern, never paying a dividend on its ordinary shares. The directors felt they had no choice but to sell up to the GWR, which duly swallowed the minnow. The East Somerset section was then converted and through-running to Witham finally began in 1878. It much improved the link with Bristol for places like Shepton Mallet, considerably reducing the journey time.

As regards motive power, services initially were operated by broad gauge locomotives; the classically named *Homer*, *Virgil* and *Seneca* were all recorded as having been used on the line. The gauge conversion brought in the ubiquitous GWR 0-6-0 saddle tanks, then for many years the GWR 45xx 2-6-2T engines had a monopoly of the passenger workings with 0-6-0 Dean Goods engines helping out with freight. GWR diesel railcars were introduced after the end of the Second World War but had disappeared by the end of the 1950s. By 1960, BR Standard class 3MT 2-6-2 tanks and Ivatt class 2MT 2-6-2 tanks were dominant, though ex-GWR Pannier tanks and Collett 0-6-0 tender engines made appearances right up to the end of passenger services. The engines mostly came from the engine sheds in Bristol at Bath Road, St Phillip's Marsh and later Barrow Road. The distance of 31¾ miles from Yatton to Witham made the line the longest GWR branch in Somerset. Passenger trains took between 74 and 101 minutes for the complete journey. Unusually, almost every train had a different time allowed. The line had a speed limit of 35 mph for passenger trains, while goods train could meander along at a more leisurely 20 mph. It was the peaceful nature of the line that brought about a brief moment of glory when a royal visit occurred. During the last war at the height of the London Blitz, following a visit to an aircraft factory in Bristol, the King and Queen sought refuge in the Somerset countryside and spent some nights on the line. To ensure they got some sleep, livestock were removed from nearby fields and sawdust was put down to deaden the footsteps of the royal guard. Passenger services on the line remained almost exclusively steam-hauled until the end, although North British Type 2 diesel-hydraulics covered one rostered turn. D6357 was one such loco, spotted in December 1962.

Though there were some cuts, passenger services remained broadly similar for most of the life of the line. On weekdays in 1963, six departures were timetabled from Yatton (with seven on Saturdays), of which four ran through to Witham, the rest terminating at Wells. All but one started from Bristol. In the return direction there were three departures from Witham (with five on Saturdays), one of which terminated in Wells. In addition there were four Up services that departed from Wells (though two of these only ran on Saturdays). All ran through to Bristol. At the Witham end, some trains ran on to Frome or Westbury. By 1963 there were no Sunday trains, just as had been the case at the start of services.

As for goods carried, the area was known for its dairy products and quantities of milk were handled by the railway, often in churns carried by passenger trains. The line was particularly busy at certain times of the year with soft fruit traffic. Lodge Hill, Draycott, Axbridge and Cheddar were the main stations for strawberry traffic. Special trains carried the fruit to markets in the Midlands and the north of England. Anemones were also sent out in quantity in the winter. Since the line ran through an area in which quarrying was one of the main industries, stone traffic was always important. In 1915, the owners of Sandford Quarry built a private link to the line just south of Sandford station. From then on, some 95% of all goods traffic out of Sandford was stone. Further east, Waterlip was important in its day, sending stone out via Cranmore. At Dulcote, east of Wells, the quarry was near enough to the line for blasting only to be permitted when there were no trains occupying the section and the single line train token and a 'blasting disc' had been sent up from Wells. Between the wars, over 300,000 tons of Mendip stone were being exported by rail annually. In the end it was the eastern sections of the ESR that were to survive, partly due to the preservation effort, but also due to quarrying. The final eastern section came into intensive use in 1970, when Foster Yeoman developed Merehead quarry and chose to transport the stone by rail.

Unlike many rural lines, the stations were reasonably well placed to serve their communities. This was true even of Wanstrow, which always looks so desolate in photographs. The trouble was the route was close to main roads that served the centres of the villages and the communities were soon to be served by frequent bus services. These were introduced in the 1920s, using vehicles left over from the First World War. The villages from Axbridge to Sandford and Banwell tended to see Weston-super-Mare as their focal point and hence used the No 43 bus service. The truth was the line was well loved but not well used. It was remarked with only slight hyperbole that at Congresbury there was only one passenger on a Saturday, 'and she had a privilege ticket anyway'. In most photographs taken of the stations in later years there is almost a complete lack of passengers. Another problem was that by the early 1960s it was not possible to book a through ticket from any of the branch stations. One had to re-book at Bristol Temple Meads, which, as the station master at Winscombe explained, was a ploy to suppress the figures for receipts. The line had always been a feeder for the main lines at either end and this was not taken into account when consideration was given to the question of closure.

Up until July 1963 there had been one train on summer Sundays from Bristol to Wells, arriving in Wells at 3.15pm and departing for Bristol at 7.20pm. The premature withdrawal of this train meant that the last day of passenger service became a Saturday, with a lot more trains to choose from, which probably suited last day passengers, especially those travelling some distance. The full list of locomotives in use on the last day was: 2268, 2277 (on freight), 3218, 3696, 41245, 82037 and D6353. Seven locomotives on one branch line in one day seems extravagant, but it must be remembered that on many trains the locomotive worked off the branch to Bristol, Frome and Westbury and was therefore not available to return on the next train for several hours. The seven engines were from five different classes, which represented far more variety than most branch lines would ever see.

In contrast to the inauguration of railway services, rail closures were rarely, if ever, commemorated officially. So on 7th September 1963, when 0-6-0 Pannier Tank No 3696 was waved out of Yatton with the last departure for Wells at precisely 8.20pm, there were none of the flags or bands or cheering that had accompanied the opening of the line. An extra carriage was not even attached, the usual two coaches being seen as sufficient. The chairman of the Parish Council was one of those present on the platform. 'I never had much occasion to use the train,' he said, 'but I thought I'd like to see her off for the last time.' This was a frequently expressed sentiment. Railwaymen had put down plenty of detonators so the train left to a series of explosions, a fusillade that was to be repeated at every station. There were three railwaymen in the locomotive's cab: the driver, Wilf Hodges of Eastville, Bristol; fireman Tony Harris, who was making only his second trip down the line; and Colin Forse of Yatton, who knew the route well and who was travelling on the trip out of sentiment. He had once been stuck down the line in the snow at Draycott in the terrible winter of 1962-3 that devastated the West Country. The guard was Bernard Still from Weston, who had done the Saturday turn on the line for the previous 15 years. People gathered on the platforms at each station, especially at Winscombe, where those in nearby houses opened their windows to cheer and wave. At the crossing point, Axbridge, many went back to Yatton behind 0-6-0 No 3218,

To Cheddar Wookey & Wells
WEEKDAYS

FROM	DEPART			RETURN FARES SECOND CLASS ONLY—TO		
	SX	S		Cheddar	Wookey	Wells
	a.m.	p.m.	p.m.	s. d.	s. d.	s. d.
CLEVEDON	11 0	1 13	2 17	2/9	3/3	3/6
WESTON-s-MARE	11 15	12 35	2 15	3/0	3/9	3/9
	noon					
CHEDDAR arr.	12 0	1 54	3 18	S—Saturdays only		
WOOKEY	12 13	2 9	3 32	SX—Saturdays excepted.		
WELLS	12 17	2 13	3 36			

Monday to Fridays   **RETURN SAME DAY**   **Saturdays**

Wells .... 4-20, or 7-0 p.m.   Wells .... 4-22 or 8-15 p.m.
Wookey .... 4-23, or 7-3 p.m.   Wookey .... 4-25 or 8-18 p.m.
Cheddar .... 4-40, or 7-18 p.m.   Cheddar .... 4-40 or 8-32 p.m.

A special ticket can be obtained on application at the time of booking which admits bearer to either Messrs. Cox's or Gough's Caves at Cheddar (but not both) or Wookey Hole Caves, at a reduced charge, payable at Cave Turnstile.   H.D.

---

also hauling just two coaches but with some 250 passengers on board. The locomotive had had some decorative white paint applied to the front by the driver, Harry Viles, at Witham before the run. He was instrumental in getting 3218 cleaned up for her last trip on the line. He was helped by the fact that the 0-6-0 was recently out of the works, following repairs after a collision with 41208 in Congresbury.

There is no doubt that if the Yatton to Wells route had ended as a 'heritage' railway it would have been known as the Strawberry Line.

Running through a holiday area from a main-line connection, it would have been a good candidate for preservation, but that was not to be. After many struggles and hard work the Cheddar Valley Railway walk was established and much of the route can now be enjoyed as a walk and cycle path.

Those who did use the line missed it when it had gone, and not just from the standpoint of convenience. As one women said, "when we travelled from Wells station we felt we were being treated like royalty". There could be no greater recommendation. Apart from regret over the closure, one's own memories of the Yatton-Witham line are all affectionate. This was partly due to the beauty of the countryside through which it passed, but mostly to the friendliness of the staff. They never showed anything other than kindly tolerance towards a young lad with his bicycle and camera. This was all the more remarkable since many of the railwaymen in the pictures were facing redundancy or having to move jobs. In retrospect, it was a privilege to have known the line and the staff in those days when, like youth, it seemed it would last forever.

The line that is the subject of our book was always known popularly as the Cheddar Valley Branch and sometimes as the Strawberry Line. To most railwaymen of the time it was the Wells Branch, even though it was not strictly speaking a branch at all, since it linked two major routes. So our trip down the line begins, as it will end, at a main-line station. From Yatton we will travel, photographically at least, across to Witham. Of the two stations, only Yatton survives. Today it no longer serves as a junction, but is mainly a busy commuter station for Bristol and Weston-super-Mare. Within living memory it was a more comfortable place to wait for trains than is the case today. There was a bookstall that survived into the 1950s and in earlier years there was a refreshment boy who sold chocolate and cigarettes. In the early 1950s there were over 40 people employed there, a number that included four locomotive crews and two shed men. The shed was situated to the west of the station and for many years was well-known for the very productive, but unofficial, vegetable plots and chicken runs adjacent to it. Behind the shed was a broad gauge horsebox minus its wheels that for many years served as a mess room for the crews and later as a store. This was originally broad-gauge territory. The Bristol & Exeter Railway opened its broad-gauge line from Bristol to Bridgwater on 14th June 1841. At that time Yatton was known as Clevedon Road, becoming Yatton when a branch was opened to the seaside at Clevedon on 28th July 1847. It took the name Yatton from a village that lay half a mile to the south. The station had mixed-gauge track from 1875 until the final conversion to standard gauge (4 8½) that took place in 1892.

The first photograph from Yatton shows ex-GWR 2-6-0 No 7332 arriving on the main line with an Up stopping train for Bristol Temple Meads in the summer of 1959. Notice the nameboard mentioning the Cheddar and Clevedon lines – the former curved to the left behind the 'parachute' water tower, the latter swung off to the right. The complexity of signalling that was required at Yatton is very noticeable in this picture. To control it all, Yatton had two signal boxes. The main one was Yatton West box (as it was known from 1925 to 1964). It had 129 levers and was in use from 14th April 1901 until 31st January 1972. Its roof can be seen behind the second coach of the train. The engine shed and signal box were both situated in the area between the Clevedon branch and the main line. The engine was one of a class always known as Moguls because of their 2-6-0 wheel arrangement. They were valiant workhorses, very numerous, and found all over the Western Region of British Railways. The design dated back to 1911, though this locomotive was one of the last batch of 20 engines of the class built in 1932 to a modified design, easily recognised by the side window cabs. Yatton is on a dead-straight, dead-level stretch of line, which means expresses travel through at some speed. The photograph was taken looking towards Weston-super-Mare and in that direction the track is straight for over seven miles.

In another photograph dating from 1959, 0-6-0 pannier tank No 9771 waits in the bay platform at Yatton with a Cheddar Line train. The bay was not always used since many branch trains ran through to Bristol and hence used the main platforms. The photograph is an interesting one since it was taken from the goods platform and therefore provides an unrestricted view of the train and many of the features of the station. The distinctive water tower is shown to good effect. It was painted cream and brown and beneath can be seen the 'fire devil' that gave protection from frost in the winter. There was quite an extensive goods yard with a 6-ton crane. The yard closed on 29th November 1965, but in its final months handled only coal traffic. In earlier years it handled quantities of mushrooms, confectionary and birdseed, all produced locally. The peak times for freight traffic on the line were the few weeks of the strawberry season. In preparation for this, the required fruit vans were collected and stored at Yatton.

Unlike the situation that was found in the branch stations, passenger numbers at Yatton steadily increased as the twentieth century progressed. The number of passenger tickets issued rose from 55,958 in 1903 to 62,245 in 1933. A later figure for 1956 recorded 96,000 passengers and 136,000 outward parcels. In addition to these there were a large number of people who used the station as they changed from the branches to the main line. Yatton still has some of its Bristol & Exeter buildings and parts of the station are still recognisably the same as they were 60 years ago, but the footbridge visible in the background of the photograph has lost its roof and the bay where trains once left for Wells and Witham is now filled-in and used as a car park. It is believed that Brunel was responsible for the design of the station buildings.

Below is a ticket issued for the last train on the line, the 8.20pm departure from Yatton on 7th September 1963.

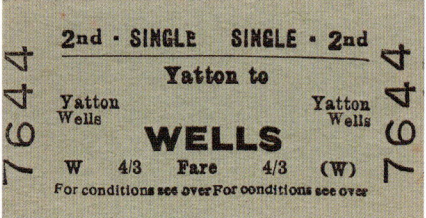

CONGRESBURY

From Yatton the line went south across flat moorland to the village of Congresbury, the name of which is sometimes pronounced 'Consbury', sometimes 'Coomsbury', and sometimes using all four syllables. The first stretch of line from Yatton was easy to construct apart from the problem of ensuring the trackbed was well drained, but shortly before Congresbury station there was call for two engineering works. A bridge was required to cross the River Yeo, immediately followed by another that carried the main Bristol to Weston road (the A370) over the railway. After the closure of the line it was soon demolished as part of a road improvement scheme.

Our first view of Congresbury shows BR 2-6-2 tank No 82007 coming into the station from Yatton with the customary two coaches on 15th September 1962, one year before the end of passenger services. The line occasionally accommodated heavy trains, such as local excursions, but these were rare. The easy run from Yatton has allowed a good head of steam to develop and the safety valves are lifting. These class 3MT tanks were ideally suited to lines such as the Cheddar Valley and the fact that none survived after the end of steam is a matter of considerable regret to the railway preservation movement today, though a scheme to build a brand-new member of the class, No 82045, for use on the Severn Valley Railway, is nearing completion. They were introduced on the Cheddar Line in 1958 and remained right to the end. The shed plate 82A denotes Bristol Bath Road depot, a main shed of which Yatton and Wells were sub-sheds.

Facing the other way (i.e. towards Cheddar), our second view from Congresbury shows another stalwart of the line, a GWR 57xx 0-6-0 Pannier Tank No 4607 entering the station before proceeding to Yatton. Again, it is hauling the two coaches that were more than sufficient to accommodate the usual number of passengers. It is a scene full of railway interest: the roof and chimney of the signal box (dating back to 1901) can just be seen behind the first coach; the goods shed with its load gauge is on the left; in front of it is a glimpse of an elderly GWR clerestory coach that had been converted to provide accommodation for holidaymakers. There were several camping coaches parked at stations along the line since it was such a popular area for visitors. The goods line to Wrington can be seen curving to the left in the distance and the splitting signal that controlled it is to the right of the goods shed. At this time (1962) closure was not certain and the station was still carefully tended with small rockeries decorating the platforms. The 57xx class pannier tanks became the standard GWR shunting and general-purpose tank engines following their introduction in 1929. They were especially numerous and at this time could be seen in large numbers all over the former GWR system. Passenger numbers were never high from the station, but goods and parcels traffic compensated. During the war, large amounts of such traffic were dealt with due to government food stores being set up locally. Over a period of time some prodigious amounts were unloaded, in particular 1000 tons of sugar. Two thousand tons of aluminium ingots were also taken into storage at one point during hostilities. In the lower right of the picture, notice the round point rodding which is pure GWR.

From 1901 Congresbury was the junction station for the branch to Blagdon that was opened on 4th December of that year. The Wrington Vale Light Railway took advantage of the Light Railways Act that reduced constructional requirements so that rural areas could be opened up to railway services. The line was reasonably successful until the start of the First World War, after which time it declined due to competition from motor transport. Passenger services ended in 1931 but freight traffic continued until June 1963. The third photograph taken in Congresbury shows No 41208 entering the station from the Yatton direction with a brake van ready to marshal the goods for Wrington. By this time, just before withdrawal of services, an occasional train sufficed. The Up platform on the left was added in 1901 and was graced by the small but particularly charming waiting room seen here. Its bay window and half-gabled roof gave it a character of its own. In the main waiting room in 1963 there were still upholstered chairs and couches carved with B&E monograms. Despite the alterations that were made when Congresbury became a junction station, passengers never benefited from a footbridge. They had to use a barrow crossing in front of the bridge where they were warned by two large notices to "Beware Of Trains". Today there is scarcely a trace of the station remaining, though the station master's house still stands. A new housing development, Station Close, is a reminder of an earlier era.

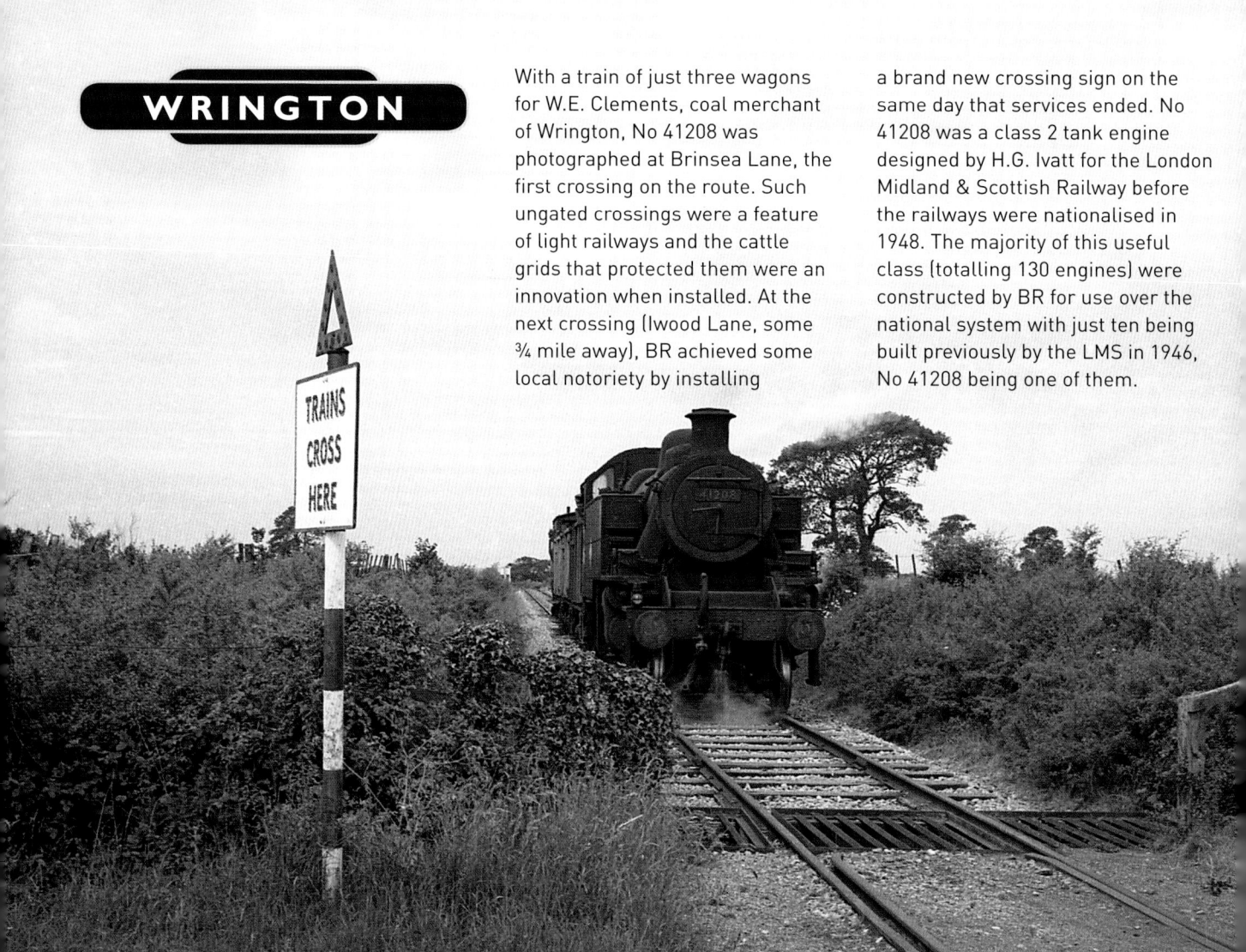

WRINGTON

With a train of just three wagons for W.E. Clements, coal merchant of Wrington, No 41208 was photographed at Brinsea Lane, the first crossing on the route. Such ungated crossings were a feature of light railways and the cattle grids that protected them were an innovation when installed. At the next crossing (Iwood Lane, some ¾ mile away), BR achieved some local notoriety by installing a brand new crossing sign on the same day that services ended. No 41208 was a class 2 tank engine designed by H.G. Ivatt for the London Midland & Scottish Railway before the railways were nationalised in 1948. The majority of this useful class (totalling 130 engines) were constructed by BR for use over the national system with just ten being built previously by the LMS in 1946, No 41208 being one of them.

USE BLOCK LETTERS 21 SEP 1961

Sender: NATIONAL COAL BOARD

East Midlands Division No. 4 Area

From SWANWICK COLLIERY

A/c

TO WRINGTON

G.W

Via W. HTH. (B) BRISTOL

WAGON Letter and Number		WEIGHT T. C.
578727	1	11-9

Description SCREENED LARGE

Consignee [GROUP 4] W.E. CLEMENTS

BM 5/4/480 R 11/56

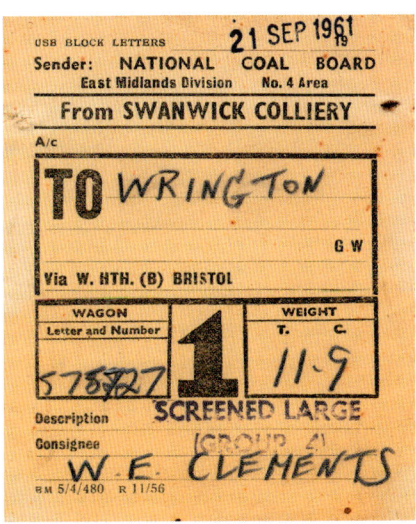

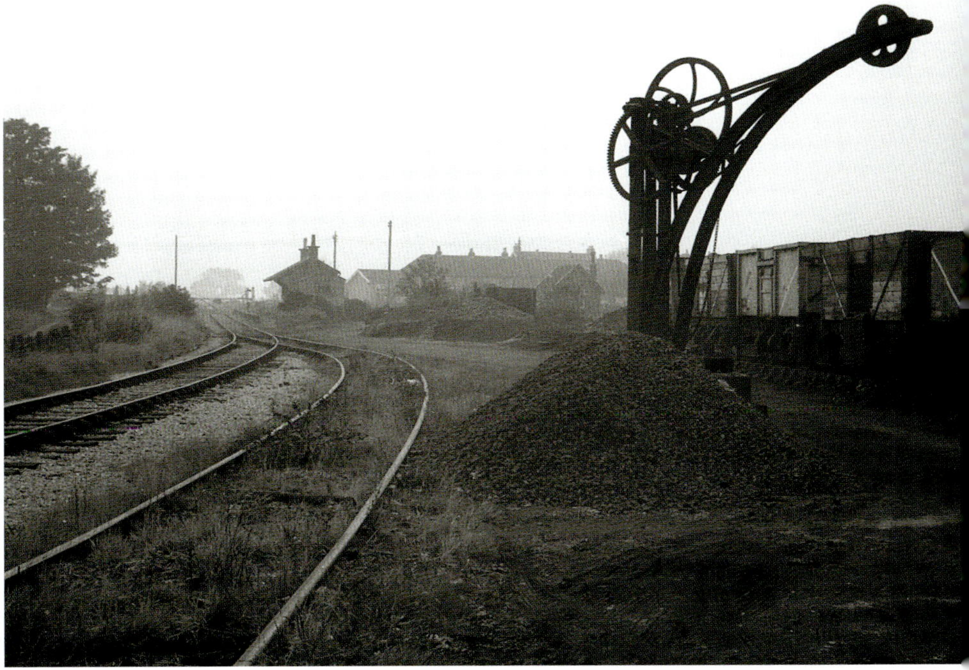

A somewhat sombre view of Wrington taken on a misty day shows the 1½-ton-rated crane and a short rake of coal wagons, two of which were of wooden plank construction. The Station Road crossing gates can just be seen to the left of the very distinctive WVLR station building. The smaller pitched-roof building in the centre housed the weighbridge office. The crane was operated by pulling on a continuous chain.

SANDFORD & BANWELL

Whilst scarcely a trace of Congresbury station can be seen today, the next station on the line fared rather better. After closure, Sandford & Banwell station was first used as a dump by the County Council before being restored in 1978 by Sandford Stone, manufacturers of ornamental garden stoneware. Latterly, as a listed building, it has become the centrepiece of a retirement village. When it became a listed building a number of specific details were mentioned. They form an excellent summary of Bristol & Exeter station architecture: snecked rubble with free stone dressings, plain clay tiles, some scalloped, crested ridge tiles; building containing waiting room, booking hall, lavatories and ancillary offices, one storey and loft; windows and doors in segmental headed openings, mainly under three large gables with very ornate bargeboards.

Unfortunately, they noted that the lean-to canopy over the platform was missing. What might have been added was that the tiles were laid with six courses of saw-tooth pattern and four of plain and the ridge tiles were topped with a small cruciform motif. In the photograph we see 2-6-2T No 41209 in the station during British Railways days. The care that the B&E took with its designs is clearly shown in the decorative windows of the goods shed seen on the right of the photograph. The care shown by the staff in the upkeep of the stations at this point is clear from the remarkable line of topiary to the left of the track. In fact, everything is spick and span and totally free of litter. The starting signal on the right is a GWR standard wooden post with a wooden arm, and looks newly painted.

There was extensive quarrying at Sandford and to facilitate transport a standard-gauge line was constructed to connect with the Cheddar branch south of Sandford & Banwell station. Sandford stone was reputed to have been used in the construction of Avonmouth Docks, opened in 1877, and in the expansion of Temple Meads Station, Bristol, in the same period (although the main walling stone was from Draycott, near Cheddar). Considerable stone traffic was always a feature of the Yatton to Witham line and this continued from Cheddar to Witham until 1969. Indeed, it continues at the Witham end up to the time of writing at Merehead Quarry by Aggregate Industries (previously Foster Yeoman Ltd). In the 1960s the firm that quarried at Sandford was Road Reconstruction Ltd. To work the short branch the company operated the 0-4-0 vertical-boilered Sentinel shunting engine seen in the illustration. Built in 1949 with works number 9391, it was photographed near the quarry where the line crossed the Sandford to Winscombe road on the level. In its heyday in the 1920s, Sandford & Banwell station was a busy place. It saw 16 passenger trains daily and an early morning milk train. Over 10,000 passenger tickets were issued annually and over 16,000 parcels processed. Average stone traffic was some 40 wagons a day, which were picked up from the exchange sidings by one of the six daily goods trains. The quarry branch closed on 30th September 1964 having provided the last traffic on the Yatton to Cheddar section of the line.

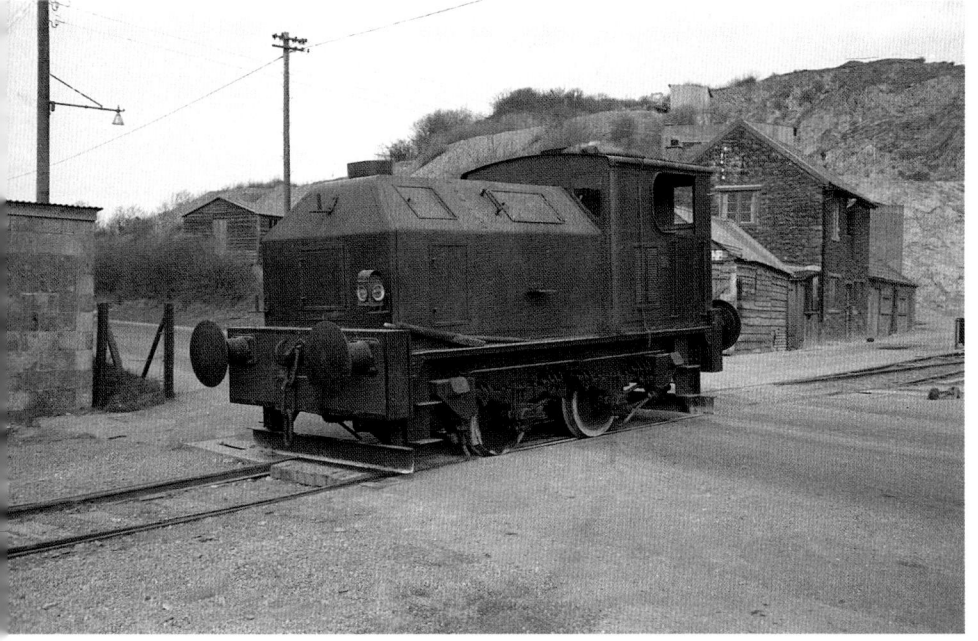

Between Yatton and Sandford the builders of the line needed few engineering works apart from the bridges at Congresbury. At Sandford they encountered more undulating ground and for the next stretch had to construct a series of cuttings and embankments. BR Standard class 3 2-6-2T No 82040 was photographed in one of the cuttings between Sandford and Winscombe on a train for Witham. Though far from clean, the locomotive is not showing a single steam leak. The track also looks in good condition, like most of the other BR lines that were soon to be closed. The hut in the distance, made of old sleepers, was for the use of the men who maintained the permanent way and was a typical feature of many rural lines.

An unidentified BR Standard class 3 2-6-2 tank was photographed as it ran into Winscombe station on a blisteringly hot summer's day in 1962. It was travelling bunker first, which was the case with half the engines seen on the line since there was no turntable available at either end, only passing loops for the engines to run round the trains. For a while there was a turntable at Witham, but it had long gone by this stage. Notice the absence of passengers; just a sack of parcels is waiting to be placed aboard.

Winscombe had two station names and two sets of station buildings. It was originally called Woodborough, but this was quickly changed to avoid confusion with another place of the same name. It was also said locally that some of the letters on the original nameboard had been fixed upside down because the man fitting them could not read, not unusual in the 1860s. The original building was a lightweight structure because of its situation on a newly built embankment. In January 1905 it was replaced by the GWR in their standard style for the period. The very few photographs that show the old station depict a small but well finished wooden building. It was eventually taken away on rollers to house a local village shop that survived for many years. Since the new station was built under GWR rather than B&E auspices, its appearance was unlike others on the line to Wells, being built of brick rather than stone and with a large roof covering the platform area. It was a single platform station with no signal box or crossing loop but had an extensive goods yard that was home to a 3-ton crane and, for a few years, a camping coach.

Immediately south of Winscombe station the railway crossed over the A371 road to Weston-super-Mare. Caught by the rays of the late evening sun, a 2-6-2 tank engine was photographed crossing the bridge as it left Winscombe with a Down train in 1963. Though the number is unknown, the slab-sided appearance of the welded side tanks and running plate mean it was certainly a BR Standard class 3. Such bridges as this were quickly targeted for demolition by local authorities keen to pursue road-widening schemes. The line's bridges, whether over or under the railway, were mostly built to the same design; they were also extremely solid, built with Mendip stone, and could prove difficult to destroy. Two attempts were required to blow up the one at Sandford. The bridge at Winscombe, shown here, had a charmed life. On the day it was due to be demolished, the contractors went into liquidation. Then, thanks to changes in local authority boundaries, it survived long enough for people to realise what a wonderful way it was to calm the traffic going through the village. It now carries walkers and cyclists along the Cheddar Valley Railway Trail.

During the summer of 1963, BR Standard 2-6-2 tank No 82037 and train were photographed from the Lynch Lane bridge, just south of Winscombe station. The locomotive was based in Bristol at Bath Road or Barrow Road sheds from January 1960 until withdrawal in August 1965. The round hill in the background is the site of the prehistoric Banwell Camp.

Between Winscombe and Axbridge lay Winscombe Hill. It was such an obstacle that it persuaded the Fox brothers to start construction of the line there. The tunnel they engineered has usually been said to be 180 yards long but has been measured more recently at 200 yards. Steam coming from the tunnel mouth can be seen in the background of the photograph of 2-6-2 tank No 82040 that was taken approximately halfway between the tunnel and the station as it approached Winscombe from the south.

As Down trains emerged from the southern end of the tunnel, passengers were treated to some exceptional views. Here we see a Collett-designed 0-6-0 running tender first down the bank towards Axbridge. The gradient was 1 in 75. In the background is King's Wood, at the north end of which was Winscombe Hall, home of the Yatmans. The embankment was built up with spoil from the tunnel.

AXBRIDGE

Once the line had crossed the A38 trunk road, on a bridge that was speedily demolished after closure, it turned east towards Axbridge. The station was approached via a deep rock cutting that can be seen in the background of the photograph. The locomotive is an Ivatt-designed class 2 2-6-2 tank running bunker first towards Winscombe. Even though closure was imminent, there is evidence of much recent track work, with platelayers being employed on maintenance right up to the last day of services. British Railways usually left its track in excellent condition for the scrap man.

This particular section was of great interest to the local transport authority, as the contemporary newspaper cutting reveals. The trackbed is now taken up by the Axbridge bypass, which was desperately needed by the village. It is ironic that when it was built the line took away the traffic that was then clogging Axbridge High Street. It was said that before the railway, 120 carts a night used to rattle through the village taking agricultural produce up to market in Bristol. Then the railway again solved modern congestion when its trackbed became a bypass.

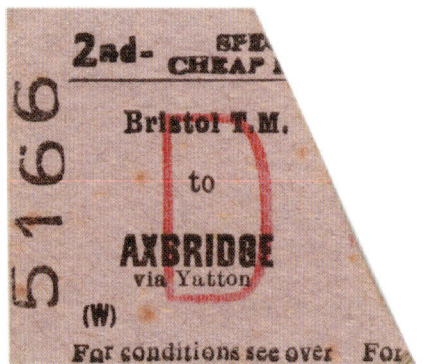

ROUTE OF AXBRIDGE BY-PASS

The line for the Axbridge by-pass is not to be decided until the future of the Cheddar Valley railway is settled, members of Somerset County Council were told.

The freight services between Congresbury and Cheddar may be withdrawn "in the foreseeable future," it was stated. If so, the line might be utilised for the new road, it has been suggested.

The Minister of Transport has deferred his decision about the by-pass until the railway's future is given. Meanwhile, the meeting at Taunton was told, a survey is being carried out to establish the advantages or disadvantages of using the railway line for the road.

The available site at Axbridge was a difficult one at which to place a station because of the hillside. There was no alternative other than building it on a ledge cut into the slope of the hill and to use the resulting spoil as a base for the goods shed and yard. The main stone buildings were on the Up (village) side of the line and were built to the usual high B&E standard. They have survived the years perfectly well and are still in use today as the Axbridge Youth Centre. The station was a crossing place for trains, as the photograph shows. Heading in an easterly direction towards Cheddar is Ivatt-designed 2-6-2T No 41208. The lifting safety valves show there is plenty of steam in reserve following the long drift down the gradient into Axbridge. The waiting shelter by the locomotive was beautifully finished with B&E bargeboards and much effort has been put into the adjacent gardens, but there are no passengers. The shelter that can be glimpsed on the left was put up to protect the strawberry traffic. The two concrete posts that can be seen supported Tilley lamps that were hauled aloft at night, a similar arrangement as existed at Winscombe. By this time, late in the life of the line, the footbridge had lost its roof. It carried a footpath leading to Fry's Hill.

Our second view of Axbridge station shows two goods trains crossing. Coming towards the camera is class 2 mixed-traffic locomotive No 46517. It carries the 82B shedplate that denoted St Philip's Marsh shed in Bristol. This 2-6-0 class was another design by H.G. Ivatt. They were introduced in 1946, after the end of the war but before the inauguration of British Railways so they were one of the last of the LMS Railway designs. For reasons now lost in the mists of time, its footplate crew would have known it as a 'Mickey Mouse'. It was clearly just ex-works and from memory was painted in BR passenger livery, which was in vogue in the Western Region at the time. It is at the head of a train hauling limestone. Interestingly, though the engines were popular with footplate crews, in tests carried out soon after the first ones were built they performed no better than the GWR Dean Goods designed more than 60 years earlier.

CHEDDAR

Two trains crossing and the exchange of tokens was the scene photographed at Cheddar near the end of passenger services in a picture that is full of interest. The goods shed to the right was decorated with the same pierced bargeboards as seen elsewhere on the line. Notice also the typically distinctive ridge tiles, the diamond ventilator and the ornate platform lamp. The locomotive running bunker first towards the camera is a BR Standard class 3 2-6-2 tank; the one on the left is a GWR Collett-designed 0-6-0, heading a train in the direction of Axbridge.

To the left of the locomotive is the original B&E signal box, still looking spick and span. It was a Saxby & Farmer Type 4 design with a hipped roof and remained in use until 3rd May 1965. A foot crossing over the tracks was provided for the signalman to exchange tokens with the crews of Down trains.

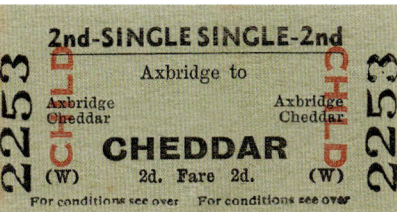

The Cheddar Valley Line 39

Cheddar had the grandest station on the route. The train shed had an impressive overall roof that needed propping up in later years. Such structures were quite a common feature of mid-Victorian GWR lines but were usually found at the terminus rather than at an intermediate station. The distance between the platforms at Cheddar was large because it had initially accommodated broad-gauge tracks. The attraction of the caves and gorge brought a considerable number of passengers in the early years and a refreshment room operated to cater for their needs. This closed in 1925 as increasing numbers of visitors chose to arrive by motor transport. It left a station that was almost embarrassingly large for its needs. As with other stations on this section of line, strawberries were important in the summer months. Passenger trains brought in the pickers from the Bristol area and goods trains took away the fruit. In the picture, the tower of St Andrew's church can be seen through the morning mist.

In the final photograph of Cheddar we see No 82009 from Bristol Bath Road shed waiting to depart at the east end of the station with a Down train, next stop Draycott. Again the absence of significant numbers of passengers is striking, as is the dilapidated state of the roof's facia. Today the station site is occupied by Wells Cathedral Stone Masons and much of the structure, though not the roof, has survived.

DRAYCOTT

Draycott station opened on 5th April 1870 with the Cheddar to Wells section. Though it was quite well positioned to serve the village, Draycott was not a very populous community and the station was never especially busy. Just 3,340 passengers were recorded in 1933. Again, it came into its own in the strawberry season and fruit boxes were often piled high on the platform. The small signal box was on the platform (seen here in the centre of the picture) and it was from there that the level crossing gates were operated using a large wheel. It was the only level crossing between Yatton and Wells. Today the station is preserved as a private dwelling. The photograph was taken in low winter sunshine in 1962 and shows BR class 3 tank No 82001 arriving with a train from the Wells direction. Just a couple of passengers are waiting.

The Standard BR tanks replaced the old stalwarts on the line, the ex-GWR 2-6-2 Prairie tanks. A photograph taken in 1949 shows one of the 45xx class, No 5547, running into Draycott at the head of its train for Yatton. Even in the earlier era there was a marked lack of passengers, the platform being filled only with empty strawberry boxes awaiting collection. The fruit formed an important source of revenue in the early summer months.

LODGE HILL

Lodge Hill station served the nearby village of Westbury-sub-Mendip. The name of the village was not used as the station name to avoid confusion with Westbury in Wiltshire. Lodge Hill was actually a small wooded hillock just to the south. As at Cheddar, the station nameboard always seemed in poor condition, unlike Draycott, which was carved deep into the stone above the main door. Despite its deserted appearance in the photograph, Lodge Hill was slightly busier than Draycott and Wookey, its neighbours. The locomotive pictured was an Ivatt class 2 2-6-2T running bunker first at the head of a train to Yatton. The small ground frame controlled access to the goods shed, which is the only railway building still standing on the site. The bridge in the distance was designed to be wide enough to accommodate two tracks should they be required. They were not.

WOOKEY

Wookey was a station of which there were great expectations that were never really fulfilled. Visitors to Wookey Hole caves and the nearby St Cuthbert's Paper Works generated some traffic, with the mill having its own siding from 1880. One of the products that came into the station in quantity was the esparto grass from which the paper was made, but it was hardly enough to justify the size of the goods shed, seen here, and by this point the track into the building looks neglected. The photograph of No 41245 was taken from the bridge carrying the road to the caves and paper mills. The train was heading for its next stop at Wells. Today, the bridge and the goods shed are the only railway structures still standing. Both were too useful to be demolished. The small signal box on the left was set forward on the platform to give signalmen a better view under the road bridge.

The Cheddar Valley Line 45

WELLS

The complicated railway history of the small cathedral city of Wells is referred to in the introduction. The last of Wells' three stations to be opened was Wells Tucker Street (just called Wells until 1920 and then again from 1951 onwards) and it was the last to close. It opened on 5th April 1870, fully 11 years after the first had opened and 8 years after the second. It was still widely known as Tucker Street in the early 1960s. In the early twentieth century, the railway staff employed at Wells totalled 80. Even in the 1940s there were some 60 employed. During the war, Wells became strategically important as a huge cold store was built there for the Ministry of Food. Just like Cheddar, the two platforms were widely spaced due to its broad-gauge legacy. This can be seen in our first photograph, which shows a handful of passengers and Collett-designed 0-6-0 No 3218 about to depart for Yatton. Trains were designated as Down (from London) from Yatton to Wells, where they then became Up to Witham.

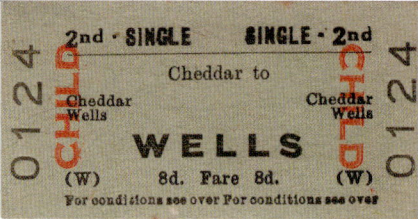

Sometimes in a railway photograph one can almost smell the steam. That is the case here, especially given the amount that is leaking from Standard class 3 tank No 82037. The driver has come down from the cab to have a word with the fireman, who is busy 'putting the bag in'. Water columns were provided between the tracks at the ends of both platforms. Water was pumped up from a convenient stream to a tank that supplied them. No 82037 was on the 8.03am Yatton to Witham and Frome and the date was 7th September 1963, the last day of passenger service. The train in the adjacent platform is the 8.22am Witham to Yatton and Bristol Temple Meads, where it was timed to arrive at 10.21am, taking 2 hours to cover 44 miles.

Class 3 tank No 82009 was in excellent mechanical condition when photographed at Wells with a train for Witham. It is a picture that shows that part of the cathedral city at its verdant best on a summer's day in the early 1960s. Though not especially clean, the locomotive's lined-out green livery can be seen. In the background on the left of the image are the covered footbridge and Burcott Road bridge. There was a small engine shed in Wells acting as a sub-shed of Bristol Bath Road. It had no engine allocation of its own nor any facilities for maintenance, being merely an overnight stabling point.

WELLS PRIORY ROAD

Priory Road station was the terminus of the line built by the Somerset Central Railway (later the S&D) from Glastonbury into Wells. Opened in 1859, this was the first of the three stations to be built in Wells by three different railway companies. When the Glastonbury branch closed, the train shed roof at Priory Road was demolished, leaving the well-constructed stone building seen here. It had been well provided with a variety of facilities, judging by the number of doors. Nearby was the site of the second station (opened in 1862), which formed the terminus of the East Somerset Railway from Witham. The third station at Tucker Street was the terminus of the line from Yatton until 1878, when through-running to Witham began. Though the Great Western had to run over a section of SCR track, with the hauteur that was perhaps typical of the company it did not deign to stop at Priory Road until 1934. So for 56 years passengers from Glastonbury who wished to use the Yatton–Witham line had to change stations in Wells. Passenger trains ceased calling at Priory Road in 1951 with the closing of the Glastonbury branch. When through-running began in 1878, the old East Somerset station became redundant. The building was then used as a cheese store but was destroyed by fire in 1929.

50   Lost Lines of England

SHEPTON MALLET

The first train into Shepton Mallet in 1858 was hauled by a broad gauge 4-4-0 saddle tank named *Homer*. As was customary, it was heavily garlanded with flowers and greeted in traditional fashion by the town band playing *See the Conquering Hero*. At that time it was the interim terminus of the line from Witham. Shepton was now 129 miles from London by rail, a journey of just over four hours. After closure, the station building survived as a depot for a cleaning company for some years. When it was decided to clear the site for redevelopment, the East Somerset Railway dismantled the structure to use for a planned 'new' station at Shepton Mallet. The first picture from Shepton dates from October 1949 and provides another opportunity to see an ex-GWR 2-6-2T of the 45xx class that were in charge of passenger services for many years. They were shorter and smaller than the other classes of GWR 'Prairie' tanks and ideally suited to the light traffic of rural branch lines. The design dated back to 1906 and was the work of George Churchward. The locomotive is in neat condition and about to depart in the Wells direction.

Trains regularly crossed at Shepton Mallet, as seen in our second photograph, dating from the mid-1950s, that shows an ex-GWR railcar with a train for Witham. The car pictured was one of the later batch that had Swindon-built bodywork with more of a razor-edge style than the earlier 'flying bananas'. Fifteen of these were specifically intended for branch and subsidiary services and were geared down to give a maximum speed of 40 mph. This was ideal for the line with its speed limit of 35 mph for passenger trains. The lower gearing enabled the rail cars to haul a tail load of up to 60 tons and a carriage is in tow in the photograph. They had a sizable luggage compartment that is being loaded by station staff while a last passenger dashes across the forecourt to catch the train. The cars were commonly seen on the Yatton to Witham line for a number of years and made a striking sight in their crimson and cream livery. Note the Down loop on the left, protected by a catch point.

In our final photograph from Shepton Mallet, the train is on the same platform but a little nearer the covered footbridge. On this occasion an 0-6-0 running tender first is providing the motive power for a Witham train. In the left foreground of the picture is a sight that may bring back some memories to readers of a certain age – the bottle of Tizer and some sandwiches that always accompanied a visit to the station. No self-respecting loco spotter went out without them and they were usually packed inside a duffel bag. The suffix High Street was added in 1949 to distinguish it from the town's other station, Charlton Road, which was some distance from the centre of town and served the S&D line. The building that can just be seen behind the carriages once housed the broad gauge locomotives of the ESR when Shepton opened as a temporary terminus before the extension to Wells was completed.

CRANMORE

Cranmore opened with the line and right from the early days dealt with limestone traffic from nearby Waterlip Quarry. Interestingly, the old quarry, now flooded, has more recently been used to test underwater explosives. Cranmore was known to railwaymen, always inclined to use nicknames, as 'Siberia'. It seemed to be in the middle of nowhere and was usually cold. Bitumen wagons continued through the station until 1985, when the traffic ceased. The station is seen here in one of those wonderfully chaotic rail tour pictures that were taken in the 1960s on 'at risk' branch lines. The tour was run by the Bristol & District Railway Society, which was started by three teenage loco-spotters standing on the end of Platform 9 at Bristol Temple Meads. The date of the tour was 15th September 1962, almost a year to the day before the withdrawal of passenger services. Cranmore was not often photographed at that time, so pictures are uncommon. It was also extremely unusual to see the platform so crowded. The sight of the DMU is rather poignant. The line was omitted from the Bristol District's dieselisation programme, which was accurately seen as an ominous sign for the future. Where the DMUs were introduced they were immediately successful and popular and had they been introduced more widely, many more lines might have been saved. Today, of course, Cranmore station is alive and well and a place where a distinctive GWR exhaust can once again be heard echoing around the Somerset countryside, thanks to the staff and volunteers of the revivified East Somerset Railway. For older visitors, it brings back memories of how things once sounded on the whole Yatton to Witham line.

WANSTROW

Wanstrow opened in 1860. The original station was very small, or at least appeared so from the track. Considerable building work was actually required at the rear to be able to have a station at the top of the embankment. The locals built it as the ESR could not or would not construct one with its own funds. In the early days the platform was so short that passengers intending to disembark at Wanstrow had to sit in the compartments nearest the guard. The driver then made sure the guard's van and adjoining coach drew up in the appropriate place. It was originally unstaffed, but in 1909 a wooden station master's office was built together with a corrugated lamp hut, both visible in the picture, which dates from 1958. A goods loop was provided in 1927.

The early-pattern GWR platform bench on the left would gladden many an enthusiast's heart today. Though it looks in a desolate spot, the station was not that far from the small community it served.

WITHAM

Witham opened on 1st September 1856 as a station on the Wilts, Somerset & Weymouth Railway, which was then just single track. It served the small but ancient village of Witham Friary. It was known as Witham for most of its life, but was renamed Witham (Somerset) under British Railways to avoid confusion with the town and station of the same name in Essex. Eight years after the change of name, BR closed the station. When the East Somerset broad-gauge line between Witham and Shepton Mallet opened on 9th November 1858, the branch trains were provided with a bay platform. This was covered with an overall wooden roof in 1870. After the closure of the line from Yatton, Witham retained services on the main line until 1966, when it was one of several village stations on that stretch to close.

In our photograph, class 3 2-6-2T No 82037 stands at the branch platform at Witham. The roof over the bay did not survive until the end of services but one of the supports can be seen to the left of the guard. The train was timetabled to arrive here at 9.34am, where it would connect with a Weymouth to Bristol service at 9.37am. No 82037 would then push its train back up the branch, cross over and then proceed up the main line to Frome at 9.45am. The guard is using a kitchen stool to rest a couple of parcels on. The shed code carried by the locomotive was 82E, which signified that it was allocated to Bristol, Barrow Road. The SC plate beneath the shed plate indicated that it benefited from a self-cleaning smoke box that reduced the work of the maintenance staff.

We end our photographic journey as we began, at a main line station. In a picture taken from the footbridge at Witham, 4-6-0 No 5932 *Haydon Hall* is seen hurtling through with an express for Taunton. The station name board denotes its status as 'Junction for Shepton Mallet and Wells', a reference back to the original destinations of the East Somerset Railway. On the right is the Down platform waiting room. It was designed by Brunel and was a sad loss when demolished. The slate-clad building on the left was the station master's house. After closure, everything was cleared and today there is little indication that there was once a station on the site. A junction at Witham remains and is heavily used for freight trains off the East Somerset line, carrying stone from Merehead Quarry.

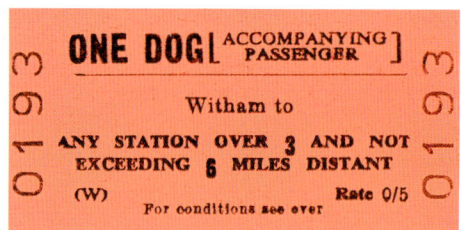

CREDITS

Lost Lines of England – The Cheddar Valley Line. Published in Great Britain in 2019 by Graffeg Limited.

Written by Paul Lawton copyright © 2019. Designed and produced by Graffeg Limited copyright © 2019.

Graffeg Limited, 24 Stradey Park Business Centre, Mwrwg Road, Llangennech, Llanelli, Carmarthenshire, SA14 8YP, Wales, UK.
Tel 01554 824000. www.graffeg.com.

Paul Lawton is hereby identified as the author of this work in accordance with section 77 of the Copyrights, Designs and Patents Act 1988.

A CIP Catalogue record for this book is available from the British Library.

All rights reserved. No part of this publication may be reproduced, stored in a retrieval system or transmitted, in any form or by any means, electronic, mechanical, photocopying, recording or otherwise, without the prior permission of the publishers.

ISBN 9781913134402

1 2 3 4 5 6 7 8 9

Photo credits
© Paul Lawton: pages 16, 18, 21, 22, 23, 25, 26, 27, 28, 29, 30, 31, 32, 35, 36, 37, 38, 40, 42, 44, 45, 47, 49, 51, 53, 55, 57.
© Norman Simmons (Photos from the Fifties): pages 12, 15.
© David Lawrence (Photos from the Fifties): page 41.
© W. A. Camwell (SLS Collection): pages 53, 54.
© Joe Moss (Roger Carpenter collection): pages 43, 59.
© Michael L. Roach: pages 48, 60, 63.

The photographs used in this book have come from a variety of sources. Wherever possible contributors have been identified although some images may have been used without credit or acknowledgement and if this is the case apologies are offered and full credit will be given in any future edition.

Cover: Yatton.
Back cover: Winscombe Hill, Sandford & Banwell, Congresbury.

Lost Lines of England series:
The Cheddar Valley Line ISBN 9781913134402
Birmingham to Oxford ISBN 9781912654871
Ryde to Cowes ISBN 9781912654864

Lost Lines of Wales series:
Cambrian Coast Line ISBN 9781909823204
Aberystwyth to Carmarthen ISBN 9781909823198
Brecon to Newport ISBN 9781909823181
Ruabon to Barmouth ISBN 9781909823174
Chester to Holyhead ISBN 9781912050697
Shrewsbury to Aberystwyth ISBN 9781912050680
The Mid Wales Line ISBN 9781912050673
Vale of Neath ISBN 9781912050666
Rhyl to Corwen ISBN 9781912213108
Bangor to Afon Wen ISBN 9781912213115
The Heads of the Valleys Line ISBN 97819126541
Conwy Valley Line ISBN 9781912654147